This NATIONAL PARKS

COLORING BOOK

belongs to

The National Parks of USA

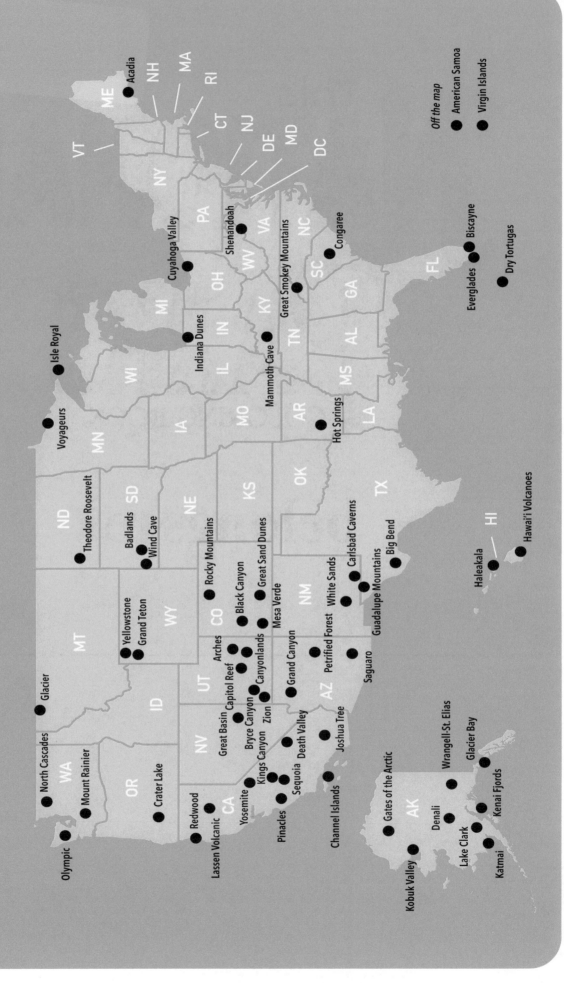

TABLE OF CONTENT

THANK YOU

We have put great care into creating this book. We hope it will provide you with many enjoyable hours of relaxation.

Feel free to leave us a comment on the Amazon product page. Your feedback is valuable. It will help others discover this book.

NATIONAL PARK AND PRESERVE

GLACIER

The park is home to over 1,000 glaciers and ice fields.

5

NATIONAL PARKS

LAKE CLARK

The park features stunning landscapes that range from
high mountains to coastal lowlands.

NATIONAL PARKS

GRAND CANYON

The Grand Canyon is one of the world's most popular tourist attractions, attracting millions of visitors each year.

NATIONAL PARKS

SAGUARO

The park is home to the iconic saguaro cactus, which can live up to 200 years.

NATIONAL PARKS

DEATH VALLEY

This park is home to the hottest recorded temperature
on Earth, which reached 134¡F (56.7¡C) in 1913.

NATIONAL PARKS

JOSHUA TREE

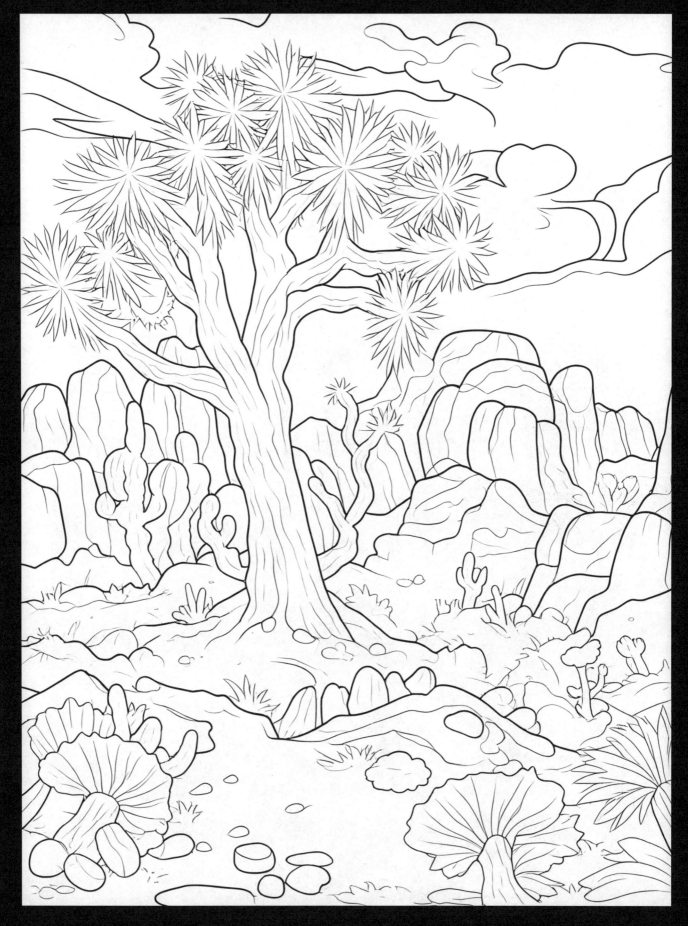

The park is named after the iconic Joshua tree, which
is only found in the Mojave Desert.

NATIONAL PARKS

The park is home to some of the world's largest trees, including the General Sherman Tree, which is the largest tree by volume.

NATIONAL PARKS

SEQUOIA

The park is home to some of the largest trees in the world, including the General Sherman Tree, which is the largest tree by volume.

NATIONAL PARKS

YOSEMITE

The park features some of the most iconic natural landmarks in the United States, including Yosemite Falls, Half Dome, and El Capitan.

NATIONAL PARKS

MESA VERDE

The park is home to some of the best preserved Native American cliff dwellings in the United States.

NATIONAL PARKS

ROCKY MOUNTAIN

The park is home to over 60 peaks that exceed 12,000 feet (3,657 meters) in elevation.

NATIONAL PARKS

HALEAKALA

The park features Haleakala Crater, which is over 7 miles (11.2 kilometers) long, 2 miles (3.2 kilometers) wide, and 2,600 feet (792 meters) deep.

NATIONAL PARKS

HAWAII VOLCANOES

The park is home to two active volcanoes, Kilauea and
Mauna Loa.

NATIONAL PARKS

ISLE ROYALE

The park is the largest island in Lake Superior and is home to a diverse array of wildlife, including moose and wolves.

NATIONAL PARKS

CUYAHOGA VALLEY

The park features over 125 miles (201 kilometers) of hiking trails and is located just a short drive from the city of Cleveland.

NATIONAL PARKS

CONGAREE

The park is home to some of the tallest trees in the eastern United States and features over 25 miles (40 kilometers) of hiking trails.

NATIONAL PARKS

WIND CAVE

The park features over 140 miles (225 kilometers) of explored cave passages and is home to one of the longest cave systems in the world.

NATIONAL PARKS

The park is home to a wide variety of plant and animal species, including over 1,500 species of flowering plants.

NATIONAL PARKS

The park is located along the Rio Grande and features stunning desert landscapes and rugged mountain peaks.

NATIONAL PARKS

GUADALUPE

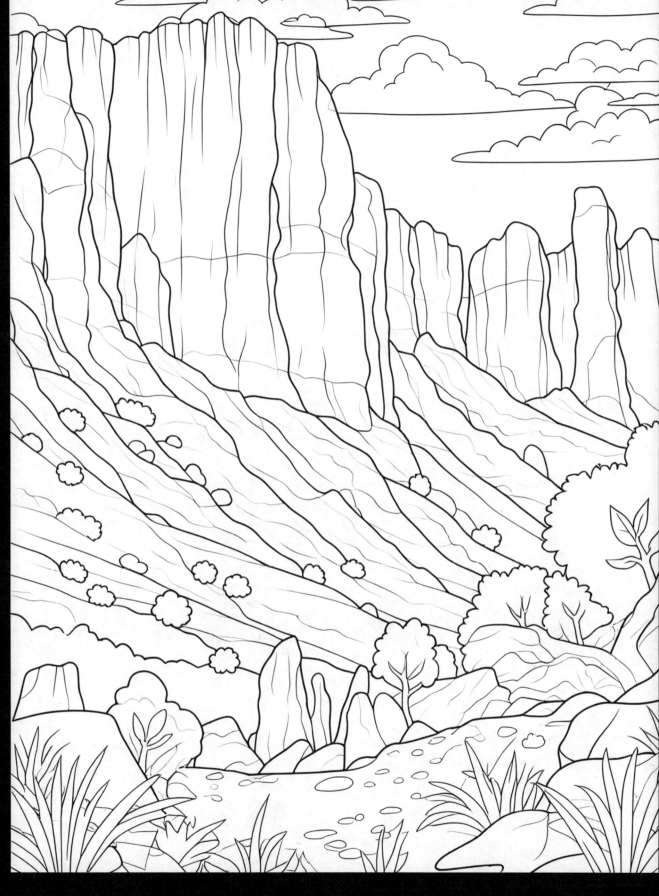

The park is home to Guadalupe Peak, the highest point in Texas.

NATIONAL PARKS

The park is home to some of the most unique
geological formations in the United States, including
hoodoos, which are tall, thin spires of rock.

45

NATIONAL PARKS

CANYONLANDS

The park features stunning desert landscapes,
including towering rock spires and deep canyons.

NATIONAL PARKS

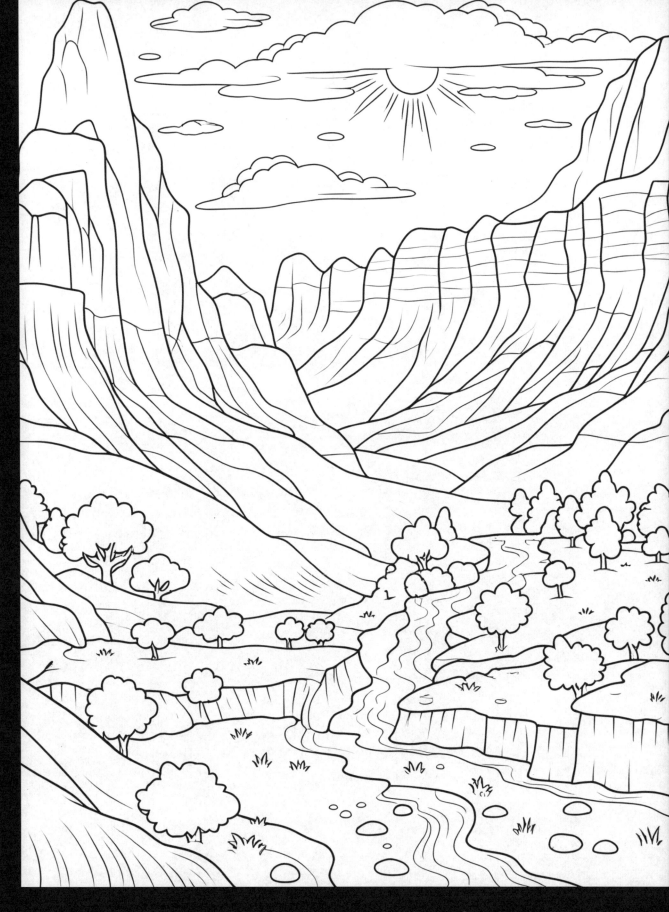

CAPITOL REEF

The park is home to a unique geologic feature known
as the Waterpocket Fold, a 100 mile (160 kilometer)
long wrinkle in the Earth's crust.

49

NATIONAL PARKS

ZION

The park is known for its towering sandstone cliffs and stunning red rock formations.

NATIONAL PARKS

SHENANDOAH

The park features the scenic Skyline Drive, a 105 mile (169 kilometer) road that offers stunning views of the park's mountains and valleys.

NATIONAL PARKS

MOUNT RAINIER

The park is home to Mount Rainier, an active volcano
that is also the highest peak in the Cascade Range.

NATIONAL PARKS

NORTH CASCADES

The park is home to over 300 glaciers and is known for
its stunning alpine scenery.

NATIONAL PARKS

The park is home to some of the largest trees in the world, as well as stunning coastal and mountain landscapes.

NATIONAL PARKS

GRAND TETON

The park is home to the stunning Teton Range and is a popular destination for hiking and climbing.

NATIONAL PARKS

YELLOWSTONE

The park is home to Old Faithful, one of the world's most famous geysers, which erupts approximately every 90 minutes.

NATIONAL PARKS

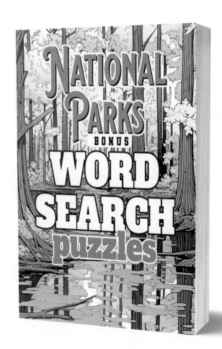

COLOR INSPIRATION GALLERY

CANYONLANDS PAGE 47

CUYAHOGA VALLEY PAGE 33

BRYCE CANYON PAGE 45

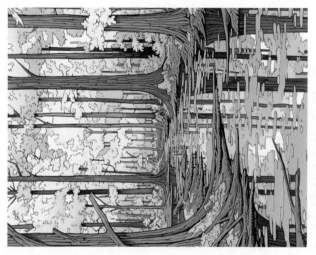

CONGAREE PAGE 35

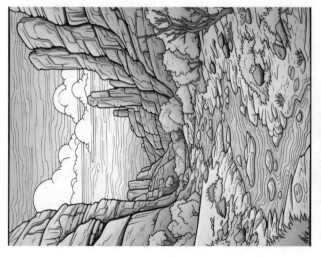

BIG BEND PAGE 41

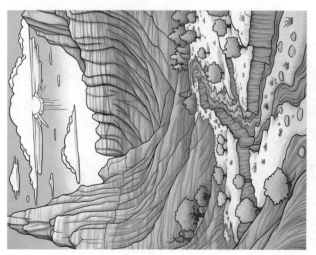

CAPITAL REEF PAGE 49

COLOR INSPIRATION GALLERY

GRAND CANYON PAGE 9

GUADALUPE PAGE 43

GLACIER PAGE 5

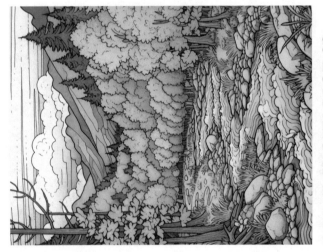

GREAT SMOKY PAGE 39

DEATH VALLEY PAGE 13

GRAND TETON PAGE 61

COLOR INSPIRATION GALLERY

ISLE ROYALE PAGE 31

HAWAÏ VOLCANOES PAGE 29

LAKE CLARK PAGE 7

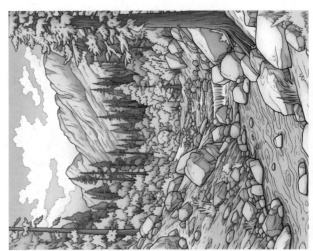

KINGS CANYON PAGE 17

HALEAKALA PAGE 27

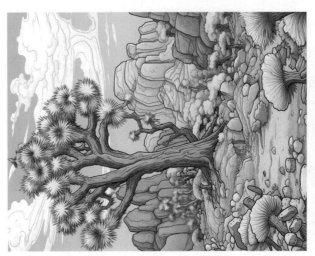

JOSUAH TREE PAGE 15

COLOR INSPIRATION GALLERY

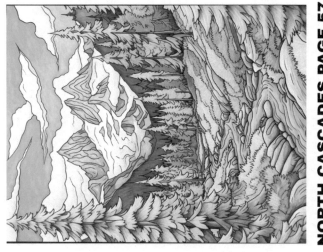

NORTH CASCADES PAGE 57

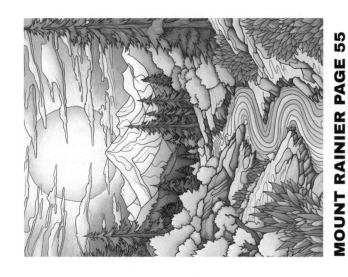

MOUNT RAINIER PAGE 55

MESA VERDE PAGE 23

SAGUARO PAGE 11

ROCKY MOUNTAIN PAGE 25

OLYMPIC PAGE 59

COLOR INSPIRATION GALLERY

WIND CAVE PAGE 37

ZION PAGE 51

SHENANDOAH PAGE 53

YOSEMITE PAGE 21

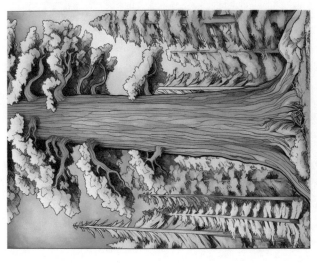

SEQUOIA PAGE 19

YELLOWSTONE PAGE 63

Made in United States
Troutdale, OR
12/28/2024

27394096R00042